The Journey to You
Danielle Scipione

FOR MY SWEET
ELEANOR

Mom and Dad spoke to me
One Sunday afternoon.
They said, "God, we are ready.
Please bring our baby soon."

I then began to work,
And thought of who you'd be.
Brown hair, curly or straight?
Tall, short, he or she?

Should your nose be like a button?
Your eyes bright like the sky?
Would you be very funny?
Quiet, loud, bold or shy?

Your parents were very kind,
In me they put their trust.
I took my time planning
As perfection can't be rushed.

Creating you took time,
I worked hard night after night,
Making you sweet as can be,
Wanting to get you just right.

A very, very long time passed

Dad was getting anxious
And Mom was feeling blue,
She spoke to me every night
- Oh, how she longed for you!

Once my work was complete
And you came one winter morn,
Everyone rejoiced
On the day you were born.

Your mom held you so tight
In fear you might not stay,
Then bowed her head real low.
"Dear God," she began to pray.

"My heart was always ready,
I've waited very long.
What were you trying to teach me?
Be brave, faithful or strong?"

I replied, "I made a miracle.
A blessing, your baby will be.
Rainbows follow storm clouds.
Struggles bring you close to Me.

Some of my children,
Take longer to create.
Life's perfect masterpiece
Is well worth the wait."

Your parents' journey wasn't easy,
But they grew along the way.
They have so much love to give you,
Today and every day.

About the Author

Danielle Scipione

M.Ed BCBA LABA

From the depths of my heart, I've always had a desire to become a mother. This aspiration stemmed from my deep love for children, my unwavering patience, and my strong connection with God. In my eyes, I felt like the perfect candidate for motherhood. Little did I know that the difficult journey of infertility would soon enter my life.

Infertility shattered my world and challenged my beliefs. It was a harsh reminder that, despite my abundant love and unyielding faith, God's divine plan doesn't always align with our own desires. This realization was a profound and often painful lesson to absorb. I struggled with emotions of anger, confusion, and a wavering faith.

Desperately, I turned to prayer with even greater intensity and duration, seeking answers and hope. At times, it felt as if God remained distant, unmoved by my pain, and unresponsive to my pleas. The years passed, marked by numerous rounds of fertility treatments, each with its own set of hopes and heartaches.

But then, the most profound blessing arrived in my life—my daughter. In that moment, my heart overflowed with joy, and my faith was rekindled. I came to understand that God had always been attentive to my prayers, although His plan was far grander and more intricate than I could have imagined.

This journey taught me that it's easy to become disheartened when God's response doesn't align with our expectations or when His timeline appears out of sync with our own. Yet, with the wisdom of hindsight, I now see that life unfolds in its own unique way, precisely as it should.

Text Copyright© 2023 by Danielle Scipione
Illustrations and artwork Copyright© 2023 by David Molinero.

First paperback edition October 2023
First Hardcover October 2023
Book design by David Molinero
ISBN 979-8-218-29159-4 (hardcover)
Published by Danielle Scipione

www.ingramcontent.com/pod-product-compliance
Lightning Source LLC
Chambersburg PA
CBRC090946120726
48010CB00013B/351